The 450 items listed in this e-book were co
business. I spent the first 10 years workin
different management jobs in a variety of o]
that time, I kept a running list of all the grea
ask and all the things I wanted to make su:
General Manager.

For the next 15 years in my career, I worked as a General Manager at 5 different luxury hotels, and then as a Regional General Manager, overseeing a portfolio of 10,000+ hotel rooms and 5,000+ employees. Throughout that time, I continued to refine the list. This book could have been titled "1000+ Things Every Hotel General Manager Should Know"! Instead, I narrowed the list down to those things that I believe will be most critical to your success as a Hotel General Manager.

This book is not intended to be *read straight through* but rather to help guide you as you focus on each of the individual areas listed. I suggest you read a few of the items, put them into practice, and then grab a few more. A mantra that has helped me throughout my career is: *Just Do The Next Thing.* Implement just one of the practices in this book, and then the next, and the next, and so forth.

Please pay particular focus to the final chapter: *Leadership and Hotel Culture.* No other information will be as critical to your success as the information in this chapter.

Please enjoy reading *450 Things Every Hotel General Manager Should Know*.

 -Marylouise Fitzgibbon, Ph.D.

CONTENTS

CHAPTER 1: OPERATING DEPARTMENTS

Housekeeping

A hotel's cleanliness is among the primary factors that impact Guest satisfaction and the overall reputation of the hotel. A General Manager should set high cleanliness standards for both the Guest rooms and the public areas, followed by constant inspections to ensure those high standards are met. Here are the items that every General Manager should know about *Housekeeping*:

1. Ensure there are clear step-by-step standard operating procedures for cleaning protocols in each area of the hotel; lobby, restrooms, common areas, fitness center, and Guest rooms. Each area should have a checklist of what gets cleaned, how it gets cleaned, and how often.

2. The GM should conduct a weekly walk of Guest rooms and public areas, on a schedule, to ensure that each Guest room and each Public Area is walked according to the schedule.

3. For public area walks, have a checklist to show all the details that must be checked (e.g., Does the clock in the fitness center have the correct time? Are the pool chairs set up properly?)

4. On each walkthrough, equip each person with a small toolkit of supplies to correct simple items on the spot. Bring furniture markers, scissors, cleaning supplies, magic erasers, carpet stain remover. There will be enough items you find that need to go on a follow-up list, so try to knock out as many small items as you can on the actual walkthrough.

5. Bring a Housekeeper on each Guest room walk that you do, so they understand the level of detail that you are looking for. During the walk, ask them for their ideas to improve cleanliness and the overall Guest experience.

6. Look at details in the Guest room from a Guests' perspective. What do they see when they lay in the bed? Stand in the shower? All the details matter here. Look under the bed, in the safe, pull out every drawer, behind the curtains, etc.

7. Put instructions on the items in the room that may not be intuitive to work (TV remotes, in-room technology).

8. Understand how the Housekeepers are audited and how often they are retrained. Ensure the training occurs in their primary language whenever possible.

9. Understand if some Housekeepers self-inspect their rooms. If so, how do you maintain quality for those rooms, and are there audits done?

10. Don't assume that every Employee has the same definition of *cleanliness*. This is an area that must be continually reinforced through training.

11. Check the cleanliness and maintenance of Housekeeping supply carts often. Ensure the Housekeepers know not to write on them or overstock them. The carts are often very visible on the Guest room floors, and they should be reflective of the care and cleanliness that you expect throughout the hotel.

12. Leverage technology to drive the productivity of the Housekeeping team. Technology can ensure that housekeepers are where they need to be and that a task, no matter how small, doesn't get overlooked. Most technology platforms update the management team, in real-time, the status of each room. This prevents your Front Desk from saying to a Guest at check-in, "let me call Housekeeping to see if your room is ready".

13. Technology should be used to understand the number of minutes it takes to clean each room type. Ensure this data is fully utilized, as it helps to control labor costs.

14. Understand if the hotel has an option for Guests to opt-out/opt-in for daily Housekeeping services. If not, consider implementing one, as not all Guests want daily service, and it's better for the environment.

15. Every hotel has some kind of ongoing challenges in the Guest rooms. The GM should know what they are and ensure there is a short-term and long-term plan to fix.

16. Know what the top Housekeeping complaints from the Guests are and have action plans in place to address each issue.

17. Understand what the Director of Housekeeping uses to track

Guestroom and lobby complaints and how they are working to fix the root causes of the top issues.

18. Get a copy of the most recent linen inventory to see if there are any issues with your par levels (3 par is typical). Understand the frequency that the inventories are calculated. This is an important step so that your Housekeepers aren't ever waiting on clean linen to get a room ready.

19. Examine the hotel's turndown service to ensure it fits your brand, and understand which Guests get it and why. Constantly look to add unexpected touches to turndown service for your Guests (eg. put a branded bookmark in their bedside book).

20. Understand the cleaning tools that are used, including chemicals, carts, and other equipment. Ensure they are each helping to achieve the cleanliness expectations while creating efficiencies and hitting cost containment goals.

21. Understand who cleans the hotel on the 3rd shift. If it is a third party, ensure walk-throughs are done with them at least once per week, so their standards are kept high.

22. Ensure that the teams who clean the public areas are well-versed in the common questions they will get from Guests.

23. Ensure that the cleaning schedule for public areas occurs at the correct times (e.g., not when Guests are departing the hotel in the morning, not when a meeting is about to break for lunch, etc.) Train those Employees to use their intuition if the plan has to change mid-day. You never want to have a 'restroom closed for cleaning' sign up. Train them to clean one stall at a time, and if someone walks in, they politely depart and come back.

24. Understand if the hotel does linen laundry in-house or if it is outsourced. Do a cost analysis to understand if it should be brought in-house or outsourced.

25. Understand how Housekeeping supplies are stored and tracked. Check the stockrooms to ensure everything is labeled and organized. Proper stock levels can have a positive influence on guest satisfaction, but there should be a process in place so that supplies aren't over-ordered.

Front Office

The hotel's Front Office is the main area Guests interact with, and the Employees in this area often set the tone for the stay. A General Manager should set high standards with this team for friendliness and follow that up with a constant presence at the Front Desk, to ensure those high standards are met. Here are the items that every General Manager should know about the *Front Office*:

26. Focus on your service standards in the Front Office. This area is so critical to the overall Guest experience. Develop a training program for the Front Office that constantly reinforces your service standards and repeat them over and over.

27. Ensure you have good technology in the Front Office that equips the Employees with the knowledge they need to exceed Guest expectations. The system should inform them if this Guest has prior stay history, any preferences, and notes about the current stay purpose.

28. Detail out the process that should occur when a Guest request comes in, and ensure the Guest is called back.

29. Understand what the protocol is when a Guest shares a complaint with a Front Desk Employee. Detail out what exactly they should do from both an empathy standpoint and a process/follow-up standpoint. Set up a tracking process so that every Guest gets a call back to ensure it was resolved to their satisfaction.

30. No calls should ring at the Front Desk. All calls should go to the back office, so that in-person Guests are never waiting for an Employee to hang up the phone.

31. Have a solid process for VIP Guests and spot-check it frequently.

32. Give all Front Desk Employees personalized business cards to hand to Guests. Connections with Guests at check-in is critically important, and personalized business cards in particular are a big win for Front Desk Employees. Have the Front Desk Employees connect with the Guests they checked in, after arrival.

33. Create an action plan for Front Desk upsells- continually refresh it to keep it exciting for the Employees.

34. Have a plan in place for how often the Front Office runs *contingency backup reports* in case the system crashes, or in the event of an emergency- and know where those reports are located. Ensure that your system flags any differently-abled Guests, so that you know which rooms to check in the event of an emergency.

35. Ensure there is a standard for what kind of pen the Front Desk Employees write with. Spot check them to ensure they are not using personal pens from home or from another business.

36. Give the Front Desk Employees luggage claim checks, so they can take luggage when the bellmen are busy. You never want to send a Guest to a different area if you don't have to.

37. Make sure you have a report that shows how often a particular Guest has stayed at your hotel. Send thank-you notes with an amenity to your frequent Guests. Amenities should change each time.

38. Guests paying especially high rates should get an amenity from the GM. Put a process in place for this.

39. Find out what supplies are commonly requested by Guests. If you do not sell them in your merchandise store, have a solid process for how to keep them handy in the Front Office.

40. Your Bellmen should ask Guests' names as they check-in and then introduce them to the Front Desk Employee.

41. Create a list of *what's happening in the city, or around your hotel* and update weekly for Guests.

42. Look at how you give Guests directions to various places. Try to get as much of this info typed out in advance, especially to places you are giving directions to frequently, so the Employee doesn't have to write it out.

43. The Front Office Manager should create a weekly newsletter for the Front Desk Employees focusing on things like:

- What to say when someone gets upgraded (to make a big win out of it)
- How to track Guest complaints
- Show Employees the positive and negative Guest comments that have come in
- Sign off-page to be attached to each newsletter to be returned to the Front Office Manager for a monthly prize drawing (a good way to see who's actually reading it)

44. Monthly Front Office meetings should be mandatory; this area is so critical to the hotel's success. The GM should get a copy of the agenda in advance to ensure the topics are equally distributed between technical knowledge and training to improve service.

45. Take your Front Desk Employees on a tour of all the subway stops leading up to your hotel or any other critical local information that Guests will need to know.

46. Train the Bell Staff to check Guests in when the lines are long. Are there any other areas that are adjacent to the Front Desk that can be trained? When you have a line at the Front Desk, you'll want a standard that everyone nearby jumps behind the desk to help. Consider putting a *lines forming at the desk* buzzer that can be pushed by the Front Desk Employees to alert the Back Office Employees to also come out and help.

47. Back Office/phone operators should have an emergency list of who to call if the elevators go down in the middle of the night or other critical issues like that. Test them often to see if they know who to call.

48. Test the Back Office/ phone operators to see how they handle various scenarios.? Create standards for the top 10 questions.

49. Ensure that your Front Office Manager is excellent at leading and motivating others. They should be constantly visible out front (not in their office), and lead by example for their team, showing how to make strong connections with Guests, and resolve problems with care and follow up.

50. GMs should be very visible at the Front Desk, and in the lobby. Carve out time on your schedule several times a day (particularly when it's busy) to be out front, visible to your Guests and your Employees.

Food & Beverage

The hotel's Food & Beverage should reflect an extraordinary experience. A General Manager should set high standards with this team for culinary and beverage creativity, followed by constant visibility and quality checks in all Food & Beverage areas, to ensure those high standards are met. Here are the items that every General Manager should know about *Food & Beverage:*

51. Get a daily shift summary from all F&B outlets (bar, restaurants, banquets, in-room-dining) so that you always keep an eye on what is happening in each area.

52. Ensure there is a weekly F&B meeting focused on both the day-to-day activities of this week but also focused on long-term revenue plans.

53. Have action plans in place for revenue generation for every one of your F&B outlets, particularly focusing on the specific time periods of need.

54. Have plans in place for increasing Guest Satisfaction for every one of your F&B outlets- know what the issues are, and what the team is doing to address every one.

55. Your restaurant should be able to stand independently of your hotel, ideally with two entrances; one through the hotel and one from the street.

56. Your restaurant manager, banquet manager, and any other area with high visibility should be present *on the floor* during all meal periods. Office time can occur in off-hours.

57. Ensure you are competing with other high-end restaurants- not other hotel restaurants.

58. Establish an outdoor dining area visible from the street, and your revenues will dramatically increase.

59. Know your food cost, beverage cost, average check, and have action plans in place to continually improve all.

60. Use technology to optimize returns in all areas by determining which menu items provide the most profit. Remove the bottom sellers and the ones that cost the most to produce.

61. Every food presentation (in the restaurant, on a buffet, or an amenity) should have a photo to show how the Chef wants it to look. Ensure these are used, or the standard will start to slip.

62. Check banquet food and setups often.

63. A good book for GMs to have on hand is *The Food Lovers' Companion.* It is updated every few years and gives a good base of knowledge of the things you should know.

64. Know how often your F&B inventories are done, and always have a copy of the most recent one.

65. If you have outsourced F&B operators, engage them by:
- Adding them to your internal email lists
- Copying them on your daily shift report
- The hotel's Director of F&B should meet with their Executive Chef and Outlet GM
- Invite them to your weekly/monthly leadership staff meetings
- Ensure that all hotel correspondence that will affect their areas is sent to their leadership team

66. Have a fast process for closing breakfast checks quickly in the morning, particularly when Guests are checking out.

67. Put a solid wine-training program in place for servers.

68. Ensure there is a great training process in place for all F&B Employees, to include upselling techniques.

69. Ensure your amenity process is documented and smooth- and understand where the process can break down.

70. When possible, work with local farmers to get items that are seasonal. Your menus should include foods that are at their peak flavor.

71. If you are among the first to do things in the world of Culinary, you will attract the best F&B Employees.

72. You want the press to pick up on your Chef and what he/she is doing that is new/different. Push your Chef to become PR worthy and not status quo.

73. Create a standard that if you have more than three items on the menu or a wine list that are 86'd (out of stock), the menu must be reprinted.

74. Understand your most recent health inspection score and what the Chef's action plan is to fix it if it was not perfect.

75. Bar experience should be focused on 5 elements: 1) Seeing (lighting, art, decoration), 2) Hearing (sound, music, conversation), 3) Smelling (scent, candles), 4) Tasting (ingredients, taste), 5) Touching (fabrics, texture).

76. Secret shop bar-cash, and let your Employees know that you do this.

77. Ensure you have solid controls in place for food and beverage items, so that nothing can *walk out* the back door.

78. Find out who has access to the liquor room, and what controls are in place.

79. In your bar, find plates that are suitable for sharing, have your Chef create opportunities for sharing food.

80. Set up clear accountability for who in F&B *owns* the Employee cafeteria; you don't want this area to be an after-thought.

Convention Services

The Convention Services department is the main point of contact for all meeting planners, who have booked a day-event, or multi-day event at the hotel. A General Manager should set high standards with this team for meeting planner satisfaction and quality offerings, followed by constant visibility in the meeting space, to ensure those high standards are met. Here are the items that every General Manager should know about *Convention Services*:

81. A convention services daily recap should be sent to the General Manager every night.

82. Have a standard that, whenever possible, any meeting room visible to the Guests should be set up when not in use so potential clients can see the space.

83. Create clear standards for every aspect of a Catering function (e.g., how servers stand in the room, what the setups should look like, etc.)

84. Check all the banquet equipment, including tables/chairs/roll-in bars, to ensure they are in alignment with your standards and not falling apart.

85. Walk the meeting space with the Director of Engineering frequently, as this area gets banged up often.

86. Create a meeting room daily checklist so that you know that all rooms are consistently being cleaned/maintained. The checklist should be turned in to a designated spot each day so it can be audited.

87. Ensure your meeting-break setups are fun and keeping up with the trends.

88. Ensure there is an easy way for Guests that use a wheelchair to get on stage in a meeting room. Don't wait until someone needs it to figure it out.

89. Ask your AV team (or whoever sets up meeting room flip-charts) to write something simple on the cover sheet of each flip-chart (e.g., welcome, an inspirational quote, etc.)

90. Always be looking for creative items to place on meeting room tables.

91. Create a standard setup for registration tables/Meeting Planner offices (e.g., stocked mini-fridge, stapler, post-it notes, etc.)

92. Train Banquet Housemen on what to say to Meeting Planners during common interactions. Don't leave this to chance, as you don't want them saying 'you'll have to go to the Ftont Desk'.

93. Train the team on how to react to Meeting Planner's last-minute changes. Solve for *yes*.

94. Standardize the process for when group overviews/resumes are distributed and ensure there is a solid resume review meeting each week with the appropriate attendees.

95. Standardize the process for Banquet Event Order (BEO) distribution and the weekly BEO meeting and ensure that Operations is involved in that process and feels they are getting accurate, timely information.

Engineering

The Engineering department is responsible for the overall maintenance of the hotel. A General Manager should set high standards with this team for ensuring every aspect of the hotel is well-maintained, followed by constant inspections of all areas to ensure those high standards are met. Here are the items that every General Manager should know about *Engineering*:

96. The GM should have a copy of the hotel's overall floorplan, including meeting rooms, Guest rooms, etc. Include the room type breakdown (how many kings, doubles, suites, accessible rooms, etc.)

97. Understand the technology that is used to track work orders for both Guest requests and internal maintenance work. Invite the vendor in to ensure everyone is trained on the full capabilities of the technology. Review the reports that the system produces to understand which areas or Guest rooms have recurring issues.

98. Review the work order backlog report monthly, looking for continual progress.

99. Ensure the hotel has a weekly Guest rooms inspection and public space inspection. The Engineer (and Housekeeping Director) should attend both.

100. Create a hotel-wide energy conservation plan and put the Engineer in charge of enforcing it. Find Employees that are passionate about environmental concerns and have them meeting monthly as part of a green team.

101. If you have a problem with your elevators or another key vendor, create a weekly meeting with them and bring follow-up notes from week to week.

102. Your service elevator should look like a Guest elevator. You may need to use it for Guests at some point.

103. Your exit stairs should be Guest-ready at all times. Guests use the stairs more than you may realize.

104. Task the Engineer (with the Director of Housekeeping at his/her side) with owning the Employee Cafeteria and all Employee back-of-house spaces. Make a list of what it would take to get these areas looking pristine and put efforts and dollars here. Ask them often for updates on how the improvements are coming along, so they know this is important to you.

105. The Engineer should be in charge of all hotel signs. Ensure no letters are missing from any signs (e.g., signs in the gym, signs by the pool, etc.)

106. Have a great Preventative Maintenance (PM) program in place. Rooms should be renewed 4-6 times a year, depending on occupancy. Keep a master list of what rooms have been done and the date. Get this process solid, including specifying exactly who must walk and sign off on a room once it's complete. The GM should walk these rooms often to ensure the rooms are meeting the standard after they are complete.

107. In addition to the PM program for Guest Rooms, there should also be one for Public Areas/Back of House/Equipment that is documented.

108. When a Guest makes a comment about a maintenance issue in a room, check to see when it was last PM'd. You may find trends of a particular Employee that is falling behind on attention to detail of the PM'd rooms.

109. Check to see what signage is used for areas of the hotel that are under construction, being painted, or broken. Nothing should be left to an Employee to create. Everything should be pre-made and on a template that is a good representation of your brand.

110. Walk your hotel with your Engineer at night to check for exterior and landscaping/lighting/signage. Things look very different at night.

111. Do not allow Engineering Employees to walk through Public Space or use the Guest elevators (e.g., Employee getting on a Guest elevator with a plunger or ladder).

112. The Engineer and the General Manager should know where all the main shut-offs are for utilities, how to reset fire alarm systems, and to detect where alarms are.

113. Set expectation that there should only be two types of Engineering work happening:

- *Unplanned Corrective-* you should have Engineers here every day for that (rooms, HVAC, kitchen, etc.)
- *Planned Corrective-* labor to work on the backlog

114. The Engineer should have a list of your vendors/contractors posted in engineering with phone numbers.

115. Ensure the Engineer knows the city codes in your locale, knows how to read utility bills, and knows those representatives.

116. Ensure everyone on all shifts has all the contact information for the Engineer in an emergency.

117. Create a process for the top engineering issues to get communicated to the GM on a monthly basis (e.g., if your top Guest complaint is AC issues, GM should know the monthly progress).

118. Ensure the fire alarm system and fire pump are tested and documented.

119. Ensure the cooling tower and other water sources are tested and documented for Legionella.

120. Ensure the pool chemical readings are tested and documented.

121. Know when all maintenance contracts expire and ensure none are on auto-renew.

122. Engineering questions every General Manager should know the answer to:
- Does the property have fan coils? If so, how old?
- Does the hotel have a 2-pipe or 4-pipe system?
- What kind of roof material does the hotel have?
- Do we have anti-vortex drains on the pool?
- What needs to be fixed/upgraded in priority order?
- Do we have an energy management system?
- Who has control of OOO rooms?
- Do we get many hot water complaints?
- What are our top engineering complaints?

- How old are the TVs & phones in the Guestroom?
- Are the major mechanicals covered under a PM program?
- Who do we use for pest control, and how often do they spray?
- What vendors do we work with- are any vendor walk-thru's needed?
- Are we ADA compliant?
- How often is our gym equipment inspected?
- Know how many risers you have and where they are. Are they straight up the building? Are they back to back?
- Do we have a recent Property Assessment?
- Get an update on OSHA regulations/ MSDS compliance / Legionella testing / Underground and above-ground fuel storage tank compliance / Pool & whirlpool drain safety standards.

123. Ensure there is a current assessment of capital needs, and if not, create one.

124. Have the Engineer walk the GM through all major mechanicals (chillers, boilers, lifts, etc.)

125. Make sure your Engineer is focused on taking the Engineering operation to the next level, not just stuck in a cycle of day-to-day maintenance.

126. In many hotels, the Engineer also oversees IT. If so, ensure they continually examine the WIFI in Guest rooms and meeting rooms to ensure it meets current customer demand.

127. Technology changes so fast; make sure there is nothing in your hotel that is outdated technology.

128. Ensure your Employees have a hotel intranet and post everything internal there.

129. Make a list of all the technology platforms your hotel has that are intended to increase speed/efficiency. Ensure everything is being used to its maximum capacity, which may mean bringing in the vendor for retraining.

130. Understand what type of phone switch the hotel has, is there a vendor that analyzes and optimizes the phone lines?

131. Understand what exactly hits the computer maintenance profit & loss line.

Security

The Security department is responsible for protecting Employees, Guests, and the assets of the property. A General Manager should set high standards with this team for safety, followed by constant visibility with the Security team and throughout the hotel, to ensure those high standards are met. Here are the items that every General Manager should know about *Security*:

132. Ensure you have a daily Security log that the GM receives each evening.

133. Put cameras back-of-house, especially by the Employee exit with signs that remind Employees that you video what leaves the hotel.

134. You should have sufficient documented mock fire drills, particularly on the overnight shift.

135. Know how the fire system works, who responds, and who monitors the system.

136. Emergency Procedures/ Fire Procedures/ Fire Drills/ Fire alarm testing- is it all up to date?

137. Have a well-stocked emergency cabinet in Security with a bullhorn, lots of flashlights, bottled water, etc.

138. Know what happens when 911 is dialed, who gets the call?

139. When a fire pull station is activated, where does the alarm call go to?

140. GMs should have copies of all emergency plans/emergency numbers.

141. In an emergency, get water & snacks to the Guests in the lobby ASAP.

142. Give lightsticks to everyone in offices in case the power goes out, and they can't see.

143. GMs should know the top Security-related complaints from Guests and Employees and what the action plans are to address.

144. Know who handles security-related trainings like CPR and First Aid.

145. Know who handles insurance claims and incident reports.

146. GM's should always be prepared in the event of a major incident. Know what to say/not say if the media shows up at your hotel after an incident:

   - In the event of a crisis, you must respond quickly (but not always on camera)
   - Never do an interview unless it's to your advantage
   - Always have your key messages ready

- If police are there, you be there too- but let the police take the lead

- Statements like "we have no tolerance for..." and "our policies are..." are good

- Often, your Corporate /Brand Public Relations team will take over but be prepared, just in case

- Generic key messages can always be: The safety and Security of our Guests are at the forefront. We are cooperating with local authorities, as this is an ongoing investigation. I am not able to comment further, but we'll be sure to update you. We're giving this great thought, we're working very hard to 'xyz,' and we'll get back to you when we know more.

Recreation

The Recreation Department oversees all areas of the hotel that Guests enjoy for leisure, such as pools, fitness center, and the spa. A General Manager should set high standards with this team focusing on creating an environment balancing fun and safety, followed by constant visibility and inspections to ensure those high standards are met. Here are the items that every General Manager should know about *Recreation*:

147. Work with your hotel's legal partner to understand what signage is necessary if your pools do not have lifeguards.

148. Ensure all areas of Recreation are safe, and no areas are accessible to children that could pose a safety threat to them.

149. Spend money sprucing up your pool and landscaping, the details matter. The landscaping must always be kept pristine.

150. Put lounging areas by the pool with outdoor pillows, don't just rely on standard pool chairs.

151. Upgrade your cabanas and include amenities that Guests actually would want and pay for.

152. Pass cold washcloths, cold water, frozen grapes, etc. around to Guests. Be creative to enhance the experience. Even if this is done just once an hour by a Front Desk Employee, it makes a big impression.

153. Look to see if you can pop up a 'splash shop' to sell hats, lotion, swimsuits, etc. by your pool, without adding additional labor.

154. Look at your pool music to make sure it matches the vibe you are trying to create. Don't leave the music selection in the hands of the Employees.

155. Ensure there are clear standards for every item in and around the pool (e.g., the rope on the lifebuoy ring should always be untangled and neatly hung, the pool chairs should be reset each night, etc).

CHAPTER 2: SUPPORT DEPARTMENTS

SUPPORT DEPARTMENTS

Finance

The Finance Department oversees the recording and reporting of financial transactions for the hotel. A General Manager should set high standards with this team for ethical reporting and control measures, followed by checks and balances to ensure those high standards are met. Here are the items that every General Manager should know about *Finance*:

156. Use data to drive decisions in the hotel. Know which metrics matter the most; Average Daily Rate (ADR), Occupancy %, Revenue Per Available Room (REVPAR), Cost Per Cover (CPC), Cost Per Occupied Room (CPOR), and keep a constant pulse check on those metrics.

157. Do an in-depth analysis of the hotel's Profit and Loss statement (P&L). Know what lies inside each line and develop plans to improve each.

158. Always look at your flow – from revenue to the bottom line. Push your team to get a better flow, every month. They should constantly be looking for opportunities for better flow without impacting service. If ADR is up, you should be able to flow close to 100% on the rate gain.

159. Understand where the daily revenue reports and daily labor reports are located and what all the department heads do with them. If you ask them random questions about items on last night's report, they will all begin to look at them more closely.

160. Look at each of your revenue-generating areas (retail shops, F&B, spa, etc.). Examine average checks, cover counts, transaction counts, for each. Constantly push for improvements in every area. Details matter here, no revenue or expense line stone unturned.

161. Know what your sales-per-occupied-room is for everything (parking, bar revenues, internet, etc.)

162. Department heads should get a monthly allotment for expenses but should not spend it all at the beginning of the month. Halfway through the month, the GM and Director of Finance should alert the teams if they need to hold back on expenses, depending on how revenue for the month is looking.

163. Look at non-value-added expenses and reduce where possible.

164. Understand how labor is managed/controlled for all areas. Labor is your number one expense. Each department should have a number of allotted labor hours each week. If any area is expected to go over hours, a process should be in place to have them explain the variance to the GM, prior to the end of the pay week.

165. Put controls in place to minimize Overtime (OT) in each area. The GM should get a weekly report of expected OT a few days before the pay week finalizes, so modifications can be made to schedules before the pay week ends.

166. Do a year-over-year analysis of your FTE's (full-time hourly and salaried headcount). Check to ensure you're not slowly increasing headcount.

167. Focus on expense control: meal break compliance, OT, office supplies, etc. by making year-over-year expense comparisons.

168. Every month, review a labor/productivity analysis by department as well as an examination of OT.

169. Understand what the hotel's cash handling policies are and how tight the checks and balances are for this area.

170. Understand what types of credit card chargebacks the hotel is receiving. Based on this, you may want to modify some of the processes at the Front Desk.

171. Conduct an accounts receivable aging review every month to ensure you understand the status of all top-dollar accounts or any accounts that are aged past 60 days. Ensure notes are taken at this meeting and start your next meeting by reviewing those notes.

172. Ensure the hotel has a tight process for looking at in-house Guest balances each day and making decisions if any Guest has a concerning high balance.

173. Understand the process the Finance department uses to approve direct billing. Is it working? Are most direct-bill accounts paying the hotel on time?

174. Look at how your hotel's name appears on Guests' American Express/Visa/Mastercard statements. Ensure it includes the hotel's phone number to reduce credit card chargebacks. If they can't figure out how to contact you to question a charge, they will just dispute it.

175. Understand the process that occurs when a Guest calls the finance office to get a copy of their folio or to get other questions answered. Set standards for response time, email verbiage used, etc.

176. Know what the top billing complaints are from Guests and put plans in place to minimize.

177. Review all audit findings- internal and external. Ensure all Sarbanes-Oxley accountability measures are in place.

178. Understand the Balance Sheet and if there are any issues.

179. Find out if there are any outstanding big-ticket items you should be aware of (workers comp pending claims, bad debt, legal billings, corporate charges, taxes, lawsuits, etc.)

180. Understand what rent & other income the hotel receives and if it is being collected according to the contracts.

181. Understand how attrition and cancelation fees are collected. Is there a good process in place to ensure it is all tracked?

182. Find out if there are solid controls in place for bar, valet and inventories. Does your hotel have secret shoppers to audit this?

183. Create a 1-page recap of all contracts/agreements, including expiration dates. Renegotiate where possible to get better terms. Contracts should not be on auto-renew and ensure that everything is occurring as it should.

184. Understand how food and beverage cost is controlled.

185. Set up an ongoing system to review accounts payable checks/ invoices. Occasionally, look at accounts payable checks before they get mailed out. Often times the department managers just sign off on expenses that they have not analyzed. There is opportunity to save money here.

186. Periodically review the finance policies to ensure the team is doing what they are supposed to and that no processes are behind schedule.

187. Know what employee incentive programs are in place, and how they are tracked.

188. When you have a month with declining revenues, send an email to your team, so they understand what the drop in revenue is and how that is impacting profit. Explain the need to control expenses, with a focus on managing overtime, only purchasing what is necessary, shed labor, encourage leader vacation time, etc. You have to react quickly when this happens.

189. If you do any special events (Mother's Day Brunches, Thanksgiving Dinners, events at the bar), do a recap (food cost, labor cost) ahead of time to find your breakeven point. Then do one after the event to see if it was financially successful. Not all events that appear to be a success when planning, actually are.

190. Keep a master binder on your desk with all your main reports (P&L, forecast, aging, etc.). You'll want it handy if an owner/asset manager/VP calls with questions.

191. Stay on top of your hotel's capital plan. Understand what projects are in the pipeline and what funding you have for them. Here is a list of things to keep in mind during a capital review:

- Know when the last time was that all your big capital items were replaced (roof, boilers, chillers, laundry equip, room renovation, public space renovation, meeting room renovation, carpets, etc.)

- Projects that have a return on investment (ROI) should be given the priority, know what the ROI is on any project that is going to generate revenue

- For every project, list whether it is for preservation of business or ROI

- Get estimates in advance of all items you are considering

- Know the materials that are in the room, or in the bathroom (marble, stone, wallpaper, etc.), as this will significantly impact the capital investment

192. Conduct a forecast review every month. Make sure you validate any increases and scrutinize any decreases. As the months actualize, check on your forecasting accuracy percentage. Have a good process in place for who schedules the meeting and who attends. Ensure notes are taken at this meeting and start your next meeting by reviewing those notes, which helps tremendously with accountability.

193. To run an effective monthly P&L meeting with Department Heads: Create an agenda. Each Department Head comes prepared with a monthly recap. The GM or Director of Finance should prepare P&L questions in advance and distribute them. Look carefully at labor, OT and expenses. Discuss all revenue-generating areas, and get into the details of number of covers for each outlet, average check, and Banquets & Catering.

194. Understand the hotel's budget cycle and have the Director of Finance create a calendar for everyone to stay on track. During the budget, set the expectation with the team that they should understand line-by-line what is being proposed for the budget. The GM should deep dive into each section.

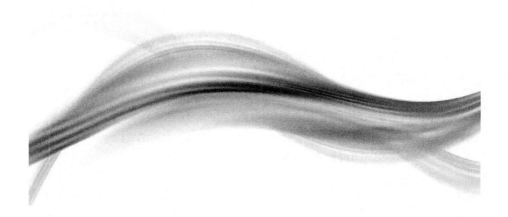

Human Resources

The Human Resources department is focused on supporting Employees throughout their employment at the hotel. A General Manager should set high standards with this team to create an excellent Employee experience, followed by continual check-ins with employees to ensure those high standards are met. Here are the items that every General Manager should know about *Human Resources*:

195. Ensure there is an overall Human Resources (HR) business plan focused on each aspect of the employee experience (recruitment, retention, training, diversity & inclusion, etc.)

196. Understand the metrics that the Human Resources Director (HRD) is measured on. Typically the HRD role has a dotted-line accountability to corporate HR, and therefore a set of key metrics they are responsible for.

197. Walk the hotel with the HR Director often, talking to as many Employees as possible.

198. Understand how your leaders are championing diversity and inclusion. The GM ultimately owns this, but the HR Director can help with the tactics. Know what the hotel's overall diversity percentage is, broken down by level (hourly, management) and department (Front Office, F&B, etc). Set a goal for improvement for under-represented groups.

199. Understand how background and reference checks occur prior to a hire and ensure there are good checks and balances prior to an Employee starting work.

200. Create a standard with the HR Director and department heads as to which new hire interviews the GM should be involved in (typically roles with high Guest-interaction).

201. Understand what the new-hire probationary period is (typical is 90 days) and ensure there is a specific process in place to evaluate a new-hire prior to the 90 days.

202. HR typically does not have a large team, so leverage Employees/Leaders throughout the hotel that want to help with various initiatives.

203. Know what tools your HR team uses to recruit, and how they get aggressive with sourcing unique, service-minded talent. Understand if they use staffing agencies for any areas.

204. Have your HRD *own* preshift meetings throughout the hotel. The HRD should train the leaders on how to run them, how to do role play, service standards, etc. They need to attend as many preshift meetings as possible. GM should attend as many as possible also.

205. HRD should ensure all leaders are doing monthly one-on-ones (these can typically be just quick, 5-10 minute meetings) with every Employee. Keep the questions structured so that you can compile the results and look for trends (eg. Tell me what's working well. Tell me what's not working well. What recurring Guest issues are you seeing and how do you believe we should fix them?) HRD should get those trends to the GM.

206. Know who is cross-trained in other areas of the hotel and if this should be amped up.

207. Understand if there is an Employee stayover program in place, and if not, consider adding one during your slow periods. Nothing trains an Employee better than having them actually experience what it's like to be a Guest in your hotel.

208. When new information comes out (e.g., a new procedure, a new standard, a new policy from the corporate office, etc.), have the HRD put it in a master pre-shift binder that goes to each area. GM should spot check occasionally that everything is actually going into each binder. If an Employee is not there for a particular pre-shift meeting, make sure each area has a plan to get the new information to them upon their return. By doing this, you can ensure that *every* employee gets *all* the same information, and nothing gets missed.

209. Challenge your HRD to champion continuous service improvement among the Employees. Review his/her action plan monthly. The GM ultimately owns service, but the HR Director can help with the tactics.

210. HR Director to champion best practice sharing. Ensure there is a process in place for a steady flow of new ideas from employees and between departments.

211. Ensure there is a tracking system in place for call-outs that each Employee has.

212. Have HR create slideshows that play in the back-of-the-house on TVs, featuring Employees. Show Mothers on Mother's Day, celebrate Cinco de Mayo, service anniversaries, etc.

213. HR to own the daily/weekly hotel newsletter.

214. Understand how training occurs for topics such as EEOC laws, disability laws, harassment policies, etc.

215. Review staffing often (key openings, diversity efforts, areas of turnover concern, outside contractor issues). Understand where the hotel uses contract labor for staffing. Question if it should be brought in house.

216. Know the Employee turnover percentage compared to the goal. Review exit questionnaires and action against any recurring issues.

217. Understand if you have any pending transfer requests from other hotels in your brand- in or out. You want to ensure Employees are not *stuck* somewhere in the transfer process.

218. Find out if there are any mentoring or Employee development programs in place, and if not, consider implementing one.

219. Get a copy of the most recent Employee survey. What is the hotel working on? Are there action plans currently in place? There should be departmental action plans and an overall hotel action plan.

220. HRD should have a plan for managing the Employee safety program, and know what the workers comp actuals to goals are. Aim for zero accidents.

221. Get a list of all Employee benefits offered and get a list of all recognition programs. Have a good communication plan for spreading the word to the Employees. Understand what your Employees like to get as rewards at this hotel (lottery tickets, grocery cards, gas cards, etc.)

222. Understand if there has been any union activity in the past year.

223. Understand the specific details around how new Employees are trained- this should be carefully mapped out for each department.

224. Get a copy of the most recent wage survey to understand if your pay rates are competitive in your local market.

225. Understand how performance reviews are done, and what the timing is. It is often less cumbersome for the team to have everyone on a common review date, rather than trickling them throughout the year.

226. HRD should champion community involvement and hotel-wide volunteer activities.

227. Create an HR monthly calendar that is focused on fun. Celebrate whenever you can (National Chocolate Day!, Bring your pet's photo and put it on the wall!, etc.)

228. Consider sending a monthly letter from the GM to the homes of each Employee. It's a great way to build a sense of pride among Employees when they can show their families all the great things happening at the hotel.

229. Understand if your hotel gets interns and if so, look at the training rotation for them.

230. Ensure the HRD works hard at being very visible to all Employees, and creates an environment with them where they feel comfortable talking to him/her about any issues.

CHAPTER 3: SALES/ MARKETING/CATERING/ REVENUE

Sales

The Sales department is responsible for driving revenue into the hotel. A General Manager should set high standards with this team for revenue expectations, followed by constant review of performance, to ensure those high standards are met. Here are the items that every General Manager should know about *Sales:*

231. GMs should spend 60% of their time in Sales, 30% in Operations, and 10% on administrative tasks.

232. When hiring a Director of Sales & Marketing (DOSM) it's best to find someone who already has the contacts and can bring you business.

233. GMs should attend the weekly sales meeting. Always know what is going on with sales.

234. GMs should attend the Daily Business Review (DBR) whenever possible. When groups are brought up in DBR, they should be producing at least a $xx group room night contribution for F&B. Figure out what this number is and ensure everyone knows it

235. Have exact DBR standards of what business needs to be brought up and what doesn't. You don't want your Sales Managers to have to wait for this meeting to quote on a booking that comes in; they should have the parameters around which business they don't need to bring up, and just book. Sales Managers should come prepared with rate, group history, stay patterns, who we're competing against, banquet contribution per group room, room rental, & minimum acceptable rate.

236. GMs should prepare for DBR and have items to discuss with your Sales Managers each time, even if it's just a 2-minute topic. Focus on things like accountability, goal setting, etc. whatever your DOSM needs your assistance with. Sales Managers have to stay motivated and driven.

237. Always push on ADR. If you can get a higher rate for your Guest Rooms, you get the correct flow.

238. GMs should occasionally attend the block/pick up meeting. This is the meeting where each group's room block/pickup is reviewed. You will want to release rooms back into inventory that do not appear to be picked up by the groups, so you don't end up with unsold inventory.

239. Each Sales Manager (Group, Catering, Transient Business,

Leisure) needs to have a quarterly action plan for their segment or market, created by the manager and reviewed/updated/approved by the DOSM. This plan should be ready to go by the first day of quarter. The plan should have specific tactics that address things like; accounts to target, sales activities, prospecting/new business development, production or closure goals, professional development. Review often.

240. Your hotel should have a few permanent site inspection rooms. First cleaned, last sold. These rooms have their own VIP cleaning guidelines. Ensure you have a standard site inspection form and use as many Employees as possible in your site inspections.

241. Look into your market mix - make sure you are tapping into specific vertical markets that have exhibited success in other *like-markets* (e.g., fashion, retail, design, technology, entertainment, legal). In a vertical market strategy, you should have a target account from each market segment so that if one market segment tanks, you don't have all your eggs in one basket.

242. Think about how to shift market mix. Look at specific accounts that may be down, analyze the problems and then create solutions.

243. Ensure you have direct sales activity against key accounts in your market.

244. The GM should read sales material. Educate the Sales Managers on the psychology of buying.

245. Understand what the Director of Sales does each week with the competitions' reader boards (the groups they are hosting this week).

246. Find out who your comp set has that you want to target. Make a list and go after them.

247. Look at *source of business* reports, so you know who is booking business into your hotel from your corporate sales offices or other booking agencies. Send those people birthday cards, anniversary cards, thank you cards, etc.

248. Get with all the hotels right around you to set up a program to get their leads if they can't take them. Host a local reception for local hotel sales teams to get to know your hotel- make it fun.

249. Create a card for group Guests to let them know that their group rate is available *pre and post dates*, this will help with occupancy on your group shoulder dates.

250. Things to know about Business Transient & Leisure Sales:

•   Find out how your Business Transient Sales Manager (BTSM) communicates with their clients. They should have them all on a BCC email distribution list and be able to send out an email blast to the group of sold-out dates, special offers, etc.
•   GM should always know who your top 20 repeat customers are
•   Always look at the volume of your accounts, and price your rate accordingly
•   LRA accounts (last room availability): look at the day of the week- are they coming when you need them to? If not, they should not be LRA, and they may be causing issues for your overall hotel stay patterns so that others can't get in
•   NLRA accounts (non-last room availability): you want as much NLRA as you can get because you can close those rate categories out when you don't need them
•   An easy way to find out what rates your competitors are giving to business transient accounts is to put the other hotel's phone number in google, then click on *advanced*

search, and then click *PDF files only*. This will show any PDF that lists that hotel and typically will show you what businesses they have negotiated rates with

251. The GM should personally visit your corporate sales offices. Most also have sales meetings that allow virtual dial-ins, get on these calls, and do something new & different each time, to make your hotel memorable for them.

252. Things to know about leading a Sales Team:

- Do a sales appreciation poster every week, celebrating something
- Send thank-you notes to the homes of Sales Managers who made their goals
- At the beginning of each year, the DOSM should prepare for the GM a sales travel calendar- so you know where your sales team is planning on going and why
- Sales Managers need to be out there finding NEW customers (must be in their quarterly action plan), not just building stronger relationships with existing customers
- Sales deployment: determine where your untapped markets are, where are you getting the most business from, where are your highest rates coming from? (usually corporate), then put your best people there- don't spend a lot of effort chasing after lower-rated business
- Ask your DOSM what their ideal deployment would look like if they were just opening up the hotel, use data to make this decision
- If your DOSM wants to add another Sales Manager, make sure it's because you have an untapped market; otherwise you just spread the pie of current customers to more people
- Encourage your sales team to not take NO from a client as the final answer- that's simply where the selling begins
- Outside sales calls- typically, it takes 5 times for a sales person to contact a client before they get the business- make

sure they are out there visiting clients often
• Understand who your competitors are getting (group, leisure, business transient, catering) that you are not- and make plans around each- set priorities for what you want and what you want to go after.
• Use holidays to take promo items to clients to remind them about your hotel
• Do not allow meetings during selling hours (not between 9-4)
• Set a goal like 5 by 5 (5 strategic calls, not cold calls, done by 5pm every day)
• Get a list at the beginning of the month of groups the team is targeting to close that month- ask them about them as the month progresses
• Post the Sales Managers' goals visibly
• Make bonus check distribution a big event
• Each month, review the Sales Manager production report to learn where the Sales Managers are at YTD. Recognize the ones that are achieving their goals.
• Understand how Sales Managers' goals are broken down month by month. If someone's not making it, ask the DOSM what the plans are- each Sales Manager should get a copy of their report at month-end
• Have your Sales Managers network with their counterparts in other cities for exposure to their top accounts
• Always know what your Sales Managers are doing so you can use it in examples: "What John did yesterday was great because...". Tell stories of your people doing specifically great things to set the bar high- never say things like, "you're all doing a great job"- it's too vague- catch people doing something right
• Sales Managers need hope. Bring quality info to them. Give them something to sell. (ie. Did you know that the tile used in the bar is one of a kind?, or Did you know that Chef Amy was the youngest Chef to ever compete in Iron Chef?)
• The GM needs to be available to help Sales Managers close

any piece of business
• The best Sales Manager is the best listener and a great problem solver- then they turn around and use that information to close the deal
• The GM should constantly be looking at Sales Managers' prospectss- say things like "if you convert 10% of these, you'll make your goals this month" so they know you are looking

253. Sales Manager goals should be based on the following:

• Entertainment/sales calls- defined as quality time with a customer on property or outside of the office that enhances a business relationship and moving the sales process
• Site inspection- defined as a prospective customer assesses the hotel as a potential host
• Prospecting call- defined as making contact with a customer proactively seeking a lead, or a referral. Measured by actually speaking with a customer or influencer and gathering pertinent information. There is a difference between a call and an attempted call. Leaving a voice mail is not a qualified call, neither is sending an email.
• Customer contact via phone- not a prospecting call, but a response to qualify a lead or follow up call to discuss moving a sale forward
• Goals should be adjusted based on account portfolio and on market and/or territory- short-term transactional sellers may not have as many entertainment or sales calls, but a higher amount of customer contact calls
• The goal is to encourage consistent behavior and not have a seller host an event to meet a quota. If a Sales Manager's goal is to entertain 2 people per week, hosting a 10 person event on the first of the month to achieve a number is not encouraging consistent behavior. Their goal should be adjusted accordingly.

254. Group Booking Pace Report:

- Depending on when your booking window is, you probably only have to look at this year and the next year
- Look at rates & revenue compared to last year and budget
- Too much slippage might mean that sales managers are playing with contracts to meet their goals in the month
- Always ask what the group's history is. Make sure blocks are netted, especially if you are going to sell out
- Validate rates with your current forecast, will you still hit it based on what your report is showing?
- Identify your need months and focus on them (ask the DOSM what their plan is, and validate that against the action plan for every sales manager)

255. Negotiated Transient Pace Report:

- This report should be compiled monthly and be given to the GM at month-end, it is the BTSM's tracking report
- Look at how each account is producing- identify trends
- Focus on any account in which the production is slipping from last year
- Look at rates
- Constantly look at your BTSM strategy; what was it, and how is it turning out mid-year?
- Look at day of week report- focus on the accounts that give you production on the days that you need it

256. Questions/Comments for the DOSM:

- Explain our overall strategies, and how do they differ from weekday and weekend?
- What is our market segmentation breakdown?
- Get a copy of the Sales Managers' yearly goals
- Get a copy of group booking pace report
- Get a copy from the BTSM of their account summary by production.

- Get a copy of stay pattern summary (by day of week)
- Get a copy of a report that shows what negotiated transient accounts are in your market – and understand why your hotel doesn't get certain accounts that your competitors do
- Who are the office buildings that most impact our negotiated transient? What are their occupancies?
- If your hotel has a cross selling program with other hotels, understand how your actuals vs. goals are for the year
- Get copies of YTD Sales Manager productivity
- Ensure you have a plan to get the wedding room blocks to actually stay at your hotel and not choose a cheaper alternative (eg. gift certificate to the bride if yours is the only hotel option given, etc.)
- Understand the site inspection process- and how you can outshine your competition
- Who assigns leads to the Sales Managers?
- What is the agenda and the parameters of DBR?
- If your hotel has corporate sellers that sit off property, get a copy of their production- and understand what percentage of their prospect business closes on average
- Is there a standard for sales prospecting (i.e. how often? when?)
- Get a copy of the sales kit that is given to clients
- How often are prospects and tentative bookings reviewed?
- What type of sales training is conducted? How often?
- How often do we have sales meetings?
- What could we/do we do when we need more space (tents, etc.)
- Do we have a Sales closing room for clients and Sales Managers?
- Do the sales managers have quarterly action plans? Get copies
- Look at deployment; how is the pie divided up? Make sure it matches the market

Marketing

The Marketing department is tasked with increasing the revenue of the hotel through advertising and promotional programs. A General Manager should set high standards with this team for creativity and target-market reach, followed by constant review of performance, to ensure those high standards are met. Here are the items that every General Manager should know about *Marketing*:

257. Marketing priorities should be: 1) market share growth, 2) revenue generation, 3) partnership growth.

258. Ensure there is a solid overall marketing plan for the hotel that is refreshed quarterly.

259. Understand who does advertising and Public Relations (PR) and if they are delivering the results you need.

260. Never stop opening- ensure you have a sustained media campaign.

261. Constantly look for things in your hotel for PR to talk about.

When there is nothing, create something. Look at cutting edge hotels for inspiration.

262. PR Priorities: you need an agency that is a good connector in the local market, that does promotions, buzz-worthy events, and brings media in. You need someone who constantly is thinking of new opportunities, looking at your marketing calendar, and inserting media-worthy ideas.

263. Roll out new Guest room packages every so often, including a local partner whenever possible, to help you promote the package.

264. Drive marketing into niche areas, like Bar/Bat Mitzvahs. Look into partnerships with local magazines, like-minded brands, etc. Get in touch with the General Managers of those areas, or the editors, not the ad sales team.

265. Create a PR plan to get more advertorials/ editorials.

266. Know what Guest offers are being promoted through your brand marketing team in the upcoming months.

267. For every holiday, get marketing to assist the operating departments to determine what the hotel will do on that day to celebrate (e.g., halloween candy at arrival, roses in the restaurant on valentine's day).

268. Ensure your marketing team understands they need to drive overall hotel revenue, not just rooms revenue.

269. The Marketing Manager should update the GM monthly with data gathered from traveler review websites on your hotel (blurb.com, flyertalk.com, TripAdvisor, etc.)

270. Once a quarter, do a full website content review to ensure everything is still relevant. Check to make sure that everything is on-brand, with no grammatical errors, and that all information is correct. Look at your competitors' websites as well.

271. Check all 3rd party websites to see how your hotel is listed (hotels.com, expedia, yelp, etc.)

272. Create a master list of all marketing offers that have been placed in market. List out exactly what you did, and what the results were, so that you can make an educated decision about whether or not you want to repeat an offer.

273. Marketing should be lock and step with the hotel's Revenue Manager to look ahead at need dates and brainstorm solutions.

274. Invite the Marketing Manager to your sales strategy meeting, so they can understand where any need periods may be.

275. Create a monthly marketing calendar and detail out everything.

276. Look at your meetings offers and see how they compares to your competition.

277. What incremental revenue can you drive through Guest reservation pre-stay messages?

278. How often are you reaching out to your past customer database with marketing offers? Don't send more than 2 offers per month, or Guests will opt out at a higher rate.

279. Marketing Manager can help your F&B team create unique items for your amenity list, particularly focusing on revenue-generating amenities for birthdays and anniversaries.

280. Create fun marketing ideas around your pool. Things like *Martini nights-* jazzed up cabanas, special menu, beach balls floating in the pool, uplit plants, etc.

281. GMs should subscribe to all local magazines that target your demographic customer.

282. Ensure your marketing manager knows the marketing team at all the local magazines.

283. Market your hotel restaurant as a separate brand from the hotel.

284. Look for opportunities to market your restaurants to your neighbors- you want to make it their first choice.

285. The press should advertise your Chef for you- come up with a plan to make this happen.

286. Look online for calendars of events- see where your restaurants can be featured.

287. Restaurants must have a separate identity from the hotel (PR agency should do that).

288. Look for opportunities to host events with partners in your F&B spaces (e.g., book signings, fashion shows, etc.)

289. Understand the role that Corporate/Brand Marketing plays in the hotel.

290. How does the Marketing Manager get *need dates* from sales?

291. What are your top performing web placements?

292. What offers do you have on your website now? What is planned for the future?

Catering

The Catering department sells and oversees food & beverage events in the meeting space. A General Manager should set high standards with this team for revenue achievement and excellence in execution, followed by constant visibility and quality checks, to ensure those high standards are met. Here are the items that every General Manager should know about *Catering*:

293. Most hotels break Banquets & Catering into two categories. *Banquets* includes the F&B functions that are associated with groups that also brought in significant rooms revenue (e.g., Company X booked half your hotel rooms and therefore has all the meeting space reserved for F&B and meetings). *Catering* includes the F&B functions that have minimal or no rooms associated with it (e.g., weddings, day meetings, etc.) However, the entire area is typically just referred to as *Catering*. The GM should be very involved with everything going on with Catering.

294. Ensure your Director of Catering has a revenue generation action plan each year that is refreshed and updated monthly. It should include strategies for driving increased covers as well as average check increases.

295. Review the most recent Catering forecast often and compare that to actuals and what is pending.

296. Review the monthly Catering booking pace report to see if you are on pace with future months' bookings.

297. Look at each segment to ensure that each is growing year over year and that an individual segment isn't masked by overproduction in another (holiday parties, weddings, corporate, etc.)

298. Ensure your Director of Catering is thinking about new revenue opportunities every year (e.g., a list of amenities that we have to upsell, new markets, etc.)

299. Review the marketing plan for all segments e.g., How do you advertise your wedding business? How are you targeting corporate clients?)

300. Ensure your AV offerings/upgrades are up to par with recent technology. If a customer has something at their home or office, those are the things at a minimum that should be in your meeting space.

301. Review the hotel's Catering Guest satisfaction scores monthly.

302. Understand what your group attendee F&B spend per night is, compared to what you have forecasted, and monitor that number throughout the year.

303. Understand how often Catering *free sell dates* are updated. These are the time periods in which Catering Sellers can freely book their functions into your meeting space without concern of taking the space from the Group Sellers. Clearly spell out the parameters.

304. How are F&B minimums determined? Are they correct in the booking system? When were they last updated? This is what the sellers use, so they don't have to ask a manager before booking something. If a group hits the minimum, book it.

305. Ensure the hotel has a solid process for collecting ancillary meeting room revenue (phone lines, power, equipment, package handling, etc.)

306. Ensure the Director of Catering knows what the top complaints are from your Guests and Employees and has an ongoing plan to address them.

307. Create a process for Client interactions- who first meets the Client in the morning- who does the turnover from sales to operations -how can the Meeting Planner control the AC?

308. Does the Meeting Planner know who to call if they need something- so they don't have to go to the Front Desk? How do you communicate that to them? (e.g., a card that each Meeting Planner gets with answers to commonly asked questions, or the business card of the Convention Services Manager).

309. Once a year do a comp set Catering comparison. Look at menus, pricing, promotions.

310. Ensure you have a good process in place for pre-events and post-events to get Client feedback.

311. The GM should meet every Client during site visits and also during their meeting. When practical, GMs should call Clients during the planning process just to check in.

312. Look at menu pricing, ask your Director of Catering for a competitive survey pricing matrix- prices should be reviewed every 6 months.

313. Review your Catering collateral. Do you have the right type/ amount? Does it communicate your message effectively?

314. Ensure your Catering website has links to floor plans, menus, etc.

Revenue Management

The Revenue Management Department leads the pricing, yielding, and selling strategy for the hotel. A General Manager should set high standards for this area tied to revenue goals and strategy creation/execution, followed by frequent metrics reviews to ensure those high standards are met. Here are the items that every General Manager should know about *Revenue Management*:

315. Understand what the Director of Revenue Management (DORM) uses to forecast and stay close enough to it to be able to influence the process. Typical reports that they use:
> -*Transient:* transient pace, trend report, STLY, STLM, transient on the books, and market segment report, how many rooms are normally picked up in the month, for the month, consider: demand, holidays, promotions. *Group:* pace report, allotment/ pickup report, historical group pace pickup, group to-be's

316. Have a standard that the only person who puts rooms out of order is the DORM- otherwise, you can lose revenue on sell out nights.

317. Save big suites for the last sells so you can get the max $'s out of them.

318. Find out what your standard is for returning deposits to Guests who cancel. The goal is to keep as much as you should, while being flexible where you should be.

319. Have the DORM send you a monthly recap with info on comp set trending. Have this info charted over time to see trends.

320. Have a standard reservation confirmation email that is sent to anyone requesting in-house reservations that is on-brand.

321. Find out what the comp set is charging over your need dates/ slow periods.

322. Once per month, have the DORM give you a summary of the transient booking channel report (summarize trends only), also have them summarize any other transient trends (e.g., here's where we are the rate leader, here's how we're trending on week-ends. Thurs is our slowest day, Mon is our busiest day, we are down 7% in rate in the following segments: x.y.z, etc.)

323. Ensure your hotel is getting its fair share of business through all channels and that there are daily shops conducted to confirm.

324. Have a set weekly Strategy Meeting:

   • DORM runs this meeting, and should have an agenda
   • Look at market segment report, and identify where you are short to forecast, and find out why? What is the plan to counteract it?
   • Look at the market segment rate- if it's dropping, why? (ie. The forecast was wrong? The group dropped suites? Did we book something in the month at a lower rate?)

- If transient rate is up, ask what they've been doing to drive rate
- STAR Report: this is an industry-standard report that most hotel brands use to measure performance against the competition. Look at trends, what days of the week are you lagging behind the comp set- what's your strategy to fix it?
- Your STAR will tell you what days of the week you need more business, so you can make that part of your strategy
- Analyze all pages of the STAR - not just the overviews

325. Each quarter, do a revenue generation brainstorm: Write *transient, group, banquet & catering* on individual flipcharts, and then brainstorm solutions to get more business.

326. Know your Sales Strategy, and match it up to what actually happens (eg. if one of your strategies is to close down all discounts mid-week, look to see if any discounts got in).

327. A simple way to drive revenue is to add more room categories, and allow the Front Desk to upsell to them.

328. Items to discuss with DORM:
- Get a copy of the revenue-by-channel report
- View the previous 2-years monthly segment data
- Get a copy of the group & transient booking pace
- Get a copy of the most recent Day STAR
- What is our YTD revpar % increase?
- Have we experimented with changing our BAR (best available rates)?
- How do the Sales Managers know what rate to quote? Is there technology that guides them?
- How often are minimum acceptable group rates updated?

329. The GM should ask questions to understand open and close restrictions in place, such as *minimum length of stays* or *closed to arrivals.*

330. Reach out to your OTA (online travel agencies) market managers to ensure your hotel is open, showing and available on their sites.

331. Understand how your hotel plays in the OTA space. How are you converting Guests who book through these channels to brand-loyal Guests?

CHAPTER 4: SERVICE EXCELLENCE

The General Manager is responsible for ensuring that every Employee in the hotel and every process in place is focused on delivering service excellence at every point in a Guest's experience. Here are the items that every General Manager should know about creating a hotel culture that is focused on *Service Excellence*:

332. Everything begins with service standards. The standards the hotel has in place will determine the quality of the service levels. If the GM has set high standards, the rest of the team will follow suit. Constantly look at data to tell you which areas of service need to be improved. Data first, then let the teams weigh in with operator-gut-feeling and intuition. Not the other way around.

333. Create standards for everything (e.g., server assistant is not just told 'hot bread on every table' it's 'the bread must be 125 degrees, and placed in the middle').

334. Ensure the training (new hire training as well as ongoing training) is focused on reinforcing the standards that have been created.

335. Create service audits for the standards and determine the frequency that the audits should happen for each Employee. This is how you know who is following the standards that have been set, and who is not. Then you can coach as needed.

336. Know who handles the hotel's Customer Service complaints that come in from your corporate office, and ensure the process is smooth so you know the Guest gets responded to quickly.

337. Know the top complaints from your Guests - always have an updated list, and action plans to address.

338. Every hotel should have a Guest Service Champion who emails the Guest Satisfaction Index (GSI) report out monthly, does a monthly GSI graph to visually show your strengths and areas for opportunity, summarizes GSI results, holds a monthly GSI meeting, understands the key drivers that drive the score, reviews individual Guest surveys with team daily and ensures all are followed up on, and creates an overall action plan.

339. Ensure there is a nightly Manager-On-Duty report and that the process is solid for who gets it and how it is followed up on.

340. On a weekly basis, look at all your Guest verbatim comments, contact the Guests who had issues to get them back.

341. Post the check-in scores in the back office, by check-in agent name. It will create positive competition amongst the team, just by the visibility of it.

342. Look for new ways to surprise & delight Guests at check-in and other areas (e.g. something the desk agent hands to kids, or add a whimsical note to dry cleaning bags).

343. The GM's message to the Employees can often be as simple as: *Smile* and *Be Friendly*.

344. Talk often to Employees about the importance of using Guest names whenever possible.

345. Focus on empowerment- do the Employees know what options they have and how they execute them? Make an Empowerment toolkit: Give the Employee a list of everything they can do and make it *easy* for them to do it do (e.g.,. how does a Bellman give a free drink? If it's difficult, it won't happen). Show them what options might be appropriate for common complaints but leave it to their discretion. If there are dollar amount limits, make it clear. Make sure they don't have to get management's approval.

346. Have each manager in the hotel working on *something* to improve service and ask them to always have at least 2 Employees working on it with them. Not only to help develop them but to help give them a sense of accomplishment when the hotel does well in that area.

347. Look for non-traditional ways to get feedback from Guests that don't like surveys (e.g., post-it-note on departure folios that states 'We think you're a perfect 10, can you say the same about us?', or 'Click this QR code to leave feedback').

348. Remind Employees that every Guest they encounter has the opportunity to fill out a survey. "Would that Guest have just given you a perfect 10 for their interaction with you?"

349. Put a sheet in the Employee back-of-house each week that lists: Whose name was mentioned on a survey, who gave us a 10, where can we improve (list comments).

350. Concierge can call Guests ahead of time, asking for special requests.

351. Call Guests the day before departure to understand how their stay was and if anything could have been improved. Discuss that feedback in your morning meeting and put plans in place to resolve all issues mentioned.

352. If your hotel has third-party employees, focus just as much on their interactions. Guests think they work for you. Don't leave this to chance.

353. Find out what *rules* your hotel has for your Guests that have been passed down over the years from Employee to Employee. Train instead to *prove the customer right* and to breakdown these rules for your Guests (e.g., an Employee should never say to a Guest "we don't allow xyz," or "you can't do xyz")

354. Identify the arrival and check-out days of the week with the most Guest complaints, often your issues come from very specific days and times. Look at staffing when you're slow- this is when the majority of your complaints happen, and when people take their eye off the ball.

355. Train your Employees that when they encounter a Guest with a problem, be the person to turn it around for them- turn it into a WOW- and give them your name in the process. Studies show that Guests who had a problem that was resolved give much higher survey scores than Guests who never had a problem at all.

356. Hold monthly mandatory training sessions- especially for Employees that have high-Guest-interaction roles. Role play standards & verbiage, brainstorm how to improve service, use stories as a powerful tool to explain good/bad Guest service. If you have physical plant issues or other non-controllable issues, train your Employees how to handle them- so they're not making up the responses.

357. Have consistent lobby coverage by a Manager during your busy times. Guests who had an issue shouldn't have to wait in line to tell the Front Desk agent.

358. The GM should occasionally make a reservation for themselves. Have the Front Desk check you in, and have the bellmen actually walk you to the room. Then head right back down and check out. Yes, they know it's *you*, but you will be amazed at what you learn.

359. The GM should attend as many preshift meetings as possible to talk about service.

360. Train Employees to pick up clues that Guests are not completely satisfied. Example: If Guest responds that their stay was 'OK' – that's a clue that they are not pleased.

361. If Guests do not have time to discuss complaints, get their number, or print a business card with the General Manager's contact information to give to them.

362. If your hotel sends Guests any kind of post-stay email message, encourage them to contact the GM with any feedback (rather than posting it online).

363. When an Engineer is making repairs in room, find a small amenity (e.g., a wrench-shaped piece of candy, or a bookmark with a funny quote) that they can leave behind, along with a note so the Guest is aware the issue has been fixed- sometimes it's not obvious to the Guest if someone came or not to handle the request they had (maybe the AC was fixed, but they can't tell).

364. Put a caged helium tank, balloon, and cards in the Front Office so the desk agents have an easy way to wow Guests who are celebrating a birthday, anniversary, etc.

365. Create a 2nd email address for the GM that can be widely distributed to all Guests and checked frequently by various managers. Post the GM email address in the Guest room, or in a goodbye thank you note left in the car, when the valet pulls it up. Find creative ways to make sure Guests know that you want to hear their feedback.

366. Don't use words that aren't real to Employees when explaining service. What exactly does *excellence* look like? Show them the behavior: here's what an *average* check-in looks like, but here's what *excellence* looks like.

367. Each department needs a visible place to post the GSI Guest verbatims from the previous week. Employees need to actually see the feedback that the Guests are giving.

368. Use stories to explain to Employees. For example, if we tell a Guest that we have excellent service, but then we can't find them a phone charger, we've missed it.

369. Put a form up in each area, to ask the Employees "what tools do you need?" It's a much simpler way to learn that you are out of simple things like soup spoons or pens, rather than relying on Employees to tell a supervisor, who then tells the manager, etc.

370. If your hotel's budget allows, hire a full-time trainer for each of your key departments, rather than someone who just does it on the side. Consistency is key.

371. Have a solid plan for new-hire training. To include certified trainers, a documented process for training, etc.

372. Ensure each area has a great training manual, that is continually updated.

373. Take the top performers in your hotel and make a list of what makes them great. Then use that as criteria to hire new people.

CHAPTER 5: INSPECT WHAT YOU EXPECT

One of the best ways for a General Manager to lead the team to excellence in all areas is to *Inspect What You Expect*. Nothing should be left to chance. Excellence in any hotel is achieved through a series of repeated messages that are communicated in a variety of inspirational ways. By physically walking the hotel often, the General Manager can spot defects quickly, and can continually set expectations with the entire hotel team. Here are some suggestions to help you *Inspect What You Expect:*

374. Walk around the hotel often- is everything perfect, clean & organized? Details matter.

375. Look at EVERYTHING at your hotel (even things like ketchup presentation, to-go packaging, etc.), do they communicate the high standards you have set?

376. Listen to anything a Guest hears (on-hold music, wake-up call recordings, elevator music, etc.) and ensure it is on-brand.

377. When you walk by a cabinet, and it is hanging off the hinges, it sends your Employees a message. If you, on the other hand, fix it immediately, you send a message. Always model the behavior that you want to see. Pick up every piece of trash on the floor anywhere in the hotel- when the Employees see you do it, they will do it also.

378. Never miss a weekly walk-through with your team. Keep the notes on the hotel's intranet so the Housekeeping/maintenance teams can keep working on them throughout the week.

379. Ensure there are no paper signs taped up in the back-of-house or front-of-house, set a standard that everything must be in a frame.

380. Take a look at every piece of collateral you give to Guests- is it on-brand?

381. Hire a mystery shopper to audit all Guest-facing areas of the hotel.

382. Look at your hotel from your neighbor's perspective; what are they seeing? Especially if they are sending business your way. Even things like your rooftop should be viewed from the adjacent buildings. Everything communicates.

383. Explain to your management team that they should put on *magic glasses* every time they walk through the hotel. *Magic glasses* force you to look at everything as if you were a Guest. It's a very different experience than hurrying through the hotel to get to the next internal meeting.

384. Every aspect of your hotel should tell the Guest what brand they are at. If you look at any area of your hotel, or of the Guest experience and you could mistake it for another brand, then change it.

385. Have a standard for how often the Executive Committee must stay an overnight at the hotel checking for standards.

386. Ensure that all Employees in the hotel know what the brand standards are, and then check for them frequently.

387. Use your frequent inspections to create a *Perfect Hotel List* at the beginning of each year. Also ask the team, "If we had unlimited $$'s, what would we spend it on?" Use that list anytime you have extra dollars, particularly if you've had a great revenue month.

388. What gets measured, gets done. Measure the things that matter, and then set up a consistent auditing process to ensure you are seeing improvement everywhere.

CHAPTER 6: LEADERSHIP & HOTEL CULTURE

Running a hotel is part science, part art. The science comes through a set of tactics, which have been described in the previous sections. The art comes through understanding the powerful role that *Leadership & Hotel Culture* play in the overall effectiveness and results of the hotel. Great leadership skills can be learned and will ultimately set you and your hotel apart from the rest, in a way that simply focusing on the tactics cannot.

389. Learn as much as you can about Servant Leadership. This management style can be taught and has consistently been shown through research to be the most effective leadership style in the hospitality industry. By creating an environment that focuses on serving your Employees, they then reciprocate by creating that same positive environment for your Guests.

390. Leadership begins with a clear vision. If the Employees of the hotel don't know where you are going and where you are trying to take them, they will have a hard time getting excited about the journey. It is especially important to have a compelling vision that provides direction and focuses everyone's energy on getting where they are headed.

391. Once the vision is clear, a GM must excel at inspiring and motivating the team. If this is not a skill that comes naturally, GMs can learn these skills through training. They are critical.

392. Every GM should be the primary champion for diversity and inclusion. Ensuring that every meeting has a variety of diverse voices represented and that an environment is created in the hotel where everyone feels included.

393. The GM should always be looking to the future to evaluate the competition, the overall market, and the Guest demographic that will be needed in the future. In order to do that, GM's need to keep a pulse on not just the hotel industry but also on understanding what Guests want before they even know it.

394. People follow great leaders because they respect them, not because they have power. Leadership doesn't come because of a title, it is earned.

395. Leadership in hotels is often about: hit the message, train, repeat, hit the message, train, repeat.

396. You cannot improve anything at an organizational level until you have credibility at an individual level, then a team level. Employees will not follow you into battle unless they first believe in you as the GM, at a personal level.

397. Great GMs do not allow themselves to become separated from the occurrences on the front line. Meetings and emails can keep your calendar full, but it is imperative that you make time to walk around the hotel and interact with Guests and Employees.

398. Get organized. Each day, there are multiple priorities, but the most productive GMs find creative ways to stay organized with their staff, projects, follow ups, and meetings with their teams.

399. Learn how to delegate effectively. As a hotel GM, your time is precious, which means you can't possibly do everything. Determine who can grow and learn from taking on new assignments, and train them according to your expectations.

400. Assign tasks and then get out of the way. Once you have trained your team and you trust that they understand what needs to be done, allow them to do their work without your interference. Micromanaging how someone does a task demotivates them.

401. Listen to your Employees. They should feel that they are truly part of the success of the hotel. Employees can offer invaluable insights on how you can run the property better.

402. Share Your Knowledge. Teaching others is a big part of a GMs job. Sharing what you know with your Employees will build a sense of empowerment while at the same time making your job easier because you're equipping them with knowledge and skills they can use to excel at their job.

403. Get to know your Employees on a personal level. Gone are the days when we asked Employees to *leave their personal issues at the door.* Lessons from great GMs have taught us that you can still have some level of professional distance, all while making sure that your Employees know you are interested in them and work to get to know them personally. Research in this area continually shows that leaders who treat their Employees as family have higher productivity and better workplace morale.

404. Make a list of each person's developmental needs and help them focus on those things.

405. Break the leaders into groups and have them brainstorm solutions to common Guest complaints or revenue generation ideas. People tend to defend that which they helped to create.

406. Create a list of what leaders need to be great at to be promoted. Don't assume that they know the skills and traits that you are looking for.

407. Set goals for each leader. Make goals about achieving results, not checking boxes.

408. Put emphasis on ensuring all leaders understand that a key piece of having a great hotel culture starts with the hires. Hire for personality, not prior resume experience. Can this Employee emotionally connect with a Guest?

409. Create campaigns featuring Employees and 'Why they love working at this hotel.'

410. Surprise and delight your Employees (e.g. in the summer after a busy week, managers stand at the Employee entrance/exit and hand out popsicles and say *thank you*).

411. Create opportunities for Employees and Managers to get together outside of work, if they choose. Volunteer events in the community are a great way to do this.

412. Create Employee pride by publicizing internally what you're doing for your Employees and for the community. Put up awards & community efforts.

413. Create a plan for leadership training to include things like monthly *lunch & learns* for the Managers, featuring different topics. Spend most of your training dollars on the leaders that directly supervise your Employees.

414. Plan quarterly Employee rallies focusing on your key messages. They should hear them over and over.

415. At your hotel's anniversary, do some sort of celebration each year.

416. Have a solid plan for Employee communication to include: daily or weekly newsletter, Employee cafeteria tent cards, pre-shifts, etc.

417. Plan activities for the overnight shift- encourage your Department Heads to visit them as often as possible. The GM should pop by the overnight shift occasionally as well, unannounced.

418. Create a positive welcome for new Employees:

- 1st day- if they work in an office, have fresh flowers, computer setup, their name is already on the phone list
- Send an email to the team 1 day prior so they all know who he/she is
- Assign the new Employee a peer and make sure someone invites them to lunch
- Take a photo of new Employees from Orientation, and post for all to see and welcome them.

419. Plan a Leader outing every quarter for team building.

420. Have a good way for Employees to get their suggestions to upper management (some may not feel comfortable talking to their leader, so come up with a simpler way for them to share information with you). You can also use this format for Employees to share safety concerns with you as well.

421. Always be looking for managers that can make lateral moves to grow personally and to benefit the hotel.

422. Treat Employee events to the same level that you would for Guests.

423. Schedule a GM Roundtable once per month. Invite a group of Employees to participate and share their feedback directly with the GM.

424. Anytime people are complaining, put 2 flipcharts up. One for the issue, one for the solution. "We're going to follow the 90/10 rule... spend 10% of our time talking about the challenges, and 90% of our time fixing them". Ask "can we control this ourselves?" Is this something we can influence?" Where can we put our limited time & energy to actually make an impact?

425. Ensure any internal meeting taking place in your hotel has a clear purpose. At the end of each meeting, do a quick review of what the action steps are. This exercise takes less than 30 seconds per person, and each person should share what they capture. Doing so will typically result in a few action steps that were missed or misunderstood. It also signals a sense of accountability. A meeting that ends without any action steps should have been an email.

426. Create a system within your hotel focused on continuous quality improvement. This simply means that you are constantly listening to your Guests, constantly looking at data on your key performance indicators, and constantly improving your standards. It is a never-ending process of improvement.

427. Any goal can be achieved if you simply break it down into a series of steps. The secret to the achievement of any goal is to just focus on this: *Just Do The Next Thing.* Focus on the process. Break down the task into small steps and then just do one small step at a time. Once you have mastered a step, move to the next, slow and steady. By focusing on the process it gives you guidance and forces you to look at just what's in front of you, and just this next step. The enemy of the process, is chasing results. Looking only at the results that you haven't quite achieved yet only serves to distract you from the process needed to accomplish your goal. Instead, by focusing on the process, you are forced to look at what's right in front of you and taking just one step at a time.

428. Focus on authenticity. What kind of person are you? What kind of imprint do you leave on the lives of others? Use your position as a GM to as a platform for making a difference in the lives of others. Chase authenticity, not approval.

429. GMs should understand the basic principles of Emotional Intelligence (EI). EI begins with self awareness and understanding how you are perceived by others. Yes, leaders need to be smart, but a differentiating factor between great leaders and good ones is emotional competence.

430. The hotel business is known for long hours, and a breakneck pace. Even so, some level of work-life-balance can be achieved. The GM should set the tone for what is expected, and what boundaries there are, so that the teams are not working 24/7.

431. Your leadership will not be defined by what you accomplish, but by why you allow your team to accomplish. To exercise true and lasting influence, empower your team, rather than over-powering them.

432. Great leaders have great relationships. Business is a series of relationships. Meeting the needs of Employees, Guests, Partners, etc. Building relationships should not be confused with socializing at work. Relationships allow you to achieve your goals through others, while also serving as a positive influence.

433. GMs should be great communicators. What are the key messages that you keep repeating over and over? Find creative ways to simplify the message, so that everyone on the hotel team understands the message and how it applies to them.

434. When dealing with conflict, GM's should approach the situation with confidence. It all starts with self-awareness. If you know you have the tendency to get easily heated up, work on it. Don't just assume that because you are the GM, your approach to conflict is the right one. Once you know what your danger zones are, you can anticipate your vulnerability and improve your response.

435. In tough times due to crisis or big changes, assure the team that you don't have all the answers, but you know that there are answers and you will figure it out. Take charge of the situation offer a plan of action, ask for support and show absolute confidence in a positive outcome. Share with the team what you do know. This builds a sense of trust and calm in the team, where they know you will come to them first with information, and that you are in control, with their best interests in mind.

436. Building a positive culture in a hotel environment is tough work. GMs should do their part to create an upbeat environment at work. Even if optimism isn't something you naturally lean towards, work on it, as people want to follow a leader that provides hope for the future and brings joy to the work.

437. Anytime you have to give constructive feedback to someone, always describe the facts of the situation without judgement. Describe the behavior, explain the outcome of the behavior, and discuss alternate actions for next time. It is far more effective to address a behavior than an attitude.

438. GMs should focus the teams on innovation and creativity.

Encourage the teams to bring you their wild ideas. It creates an environment where people dream big, and think of new solutions to challenges.

439. Be a great listener. Your highest priority can't be expressing your ideas and convincing others to buy into them. Listening is one of the core habits of leaders who connect with their people. Don't interrupt when others are talking. When they are done, ask questions to push for greater clarity, or deeper context.

440. Know the difference between being a manager versus a leader. Managers manage *things* (budgets, payroll, issues, schedules), but leaders lead *people* (listening, teaching, guiding). Leadership doesn't come from a position or a title, it must be earned.

441. Focus on motivating and inspiring the team. Simplicity often trumps grand gestures. Send employees notes that say "I continue to hear your name, thank you for all you are doing". Send it to their homes so their families can see. Recognize Employees wherever possible.

442. GMs should be able to effectively lead change. This doesn't mean you have to naturally love change, but it does mean that you learn the skills to lead change and adapt quickly, versus resisting.

443. Have an *outside-in* view of your hotel, not an *insideout* view. This means that you keep your finger on the pulse of what is happening inside your hotel, but you are even more focused on the shifting dynamics around you, so that you set your hotel and your Employees up for success in the future.

444. Be a data-driven-leader: Know what key-performance-indicators (KPIs) matter and how each is trending. The four stages of data analytics that are important for GMs to know are: *Descriptive:* information that tells you what has already happened, *Diagnostics:* look for relationships in the data, *Predictive:* using what you have learned to decide what might happen, and *Prescriptive*: using all that information to decide what course of action you should take.

445. GMs should be strategic. This means that you not only need to define the strategy for the hotel, but you need to be equally focused on executing that strategy.by translating what's written on a document into appropriate tactics.

446. Be great at asking questions. Focus on things like: What do I need to know?, Why do we have this problem?, How do we solve this problem?, What do you think?

447. Focus on building the self-esteem of everyone throughout the hotel. Research continues to show a strong connection between an Employee's self-esteem, and their job satisfaction.

448. GMs should focus on their own self-care. Corporate life can by synonymous with sacrifice, often of the mental and physical kind. Health and work don't have to be mutually exclusive. In order to operate at your best and effectively lead the team, you must optimize your health by making good food choices, exercising, cutting down on sugar, drinking plenty of water, and generally reducing stress levels. By focusing on your own self-care, it sets the example for your team to do the same.

449. Focus on showing up as your best self. This means holding yourself to the highest standards, having a strong circle of influence, and having a positive mindset. Always be fully prepared, and outwork, outlearn others. Be the one to have fun and bring the joy. Serve others and make a difference in their lives.

450. And finally, remember that small things really do make a big difference. As you finish this book, remember that the best way to start is to implement just one of the practices in this book, and then the next, and the next, and so forth. ***Just Do The Next Thing.***

*Thank you for reading **450 Things Every Hotel General Manager Should Know**. Best of luck to you on your leadership journey.*

For more leadership tips, please visit my website at: MarylouiseFitzgibbon.com

Printed in Great Britain
by Amazon

27091116R00050